Kids' Guide to Government

UNDERSTANDING HOW YOU CAN HELP

By Emma Carlson Berne

Consultant: Steven S. Smith, PhD
Professor of Political Science
Washington University

CAPSTONE PRESS
a capstone imprint

Fact Finders Books are published by Capstone Press,
1710 Roe Crest Drive, North Mankato, Minnesota 56003
www.mycapstone.com

Library of Congress Cataloging-in-Publication Data
Library of Congress Cataloging-in-Publication data is available on the Library
of Congress website.
ISBN 978-1-5435-0316-6 (library binding)
ISBN 978-1-5435-0320-3 (paperback)
ISBN 978-1-5435-0324-1 (eBook PDF)

Editorial Credits
Michelle Hasselius, editor; Mackenzie Lopez, designer;
Jo Miller, media researcher; Kathy McColley, production specialist

Photo Credits
Alamy: Shelly Rivoli, 17; Getty Images: Astrid Riecken/Stringer, 12, Bettmann/
Contributor, 15, 16, 19, The Washington Post/Contributor, 18; Newscom:
Blend Images/Betty Mallorca/Hill Street Studios, 23, Blend Images/
Eric Raptosh/Hill Street Studios, 21, Blend Images/Marc Romanelli, 27;
Shutterstock: Colorlife, 5, espies, cover, Iconic Bestiary, 25, magic pictures, 28,
Michael Candelori, 9, NKuvshinov, 26, NotionPic, 22, Sentavio, 24, Snopek
Nadia, 6, stock_photo_world, 11, Todd Kuhns, 10, Tomacco, 13

Design Elements
Capstone

Printed and bound in Canada.
010801S18

TABLE OF CONTENTS

Chapter 1
Civic Duty and Civic Responsibility 4

Chapter 2
Civic Responsibility in Action 8

Chapter 3
Civic Responsibility Champions 14

Chapter 4
What Can You Do? 20

Glossary 30

Critical Thinking Questions 31

Read More 31

Internet Sites 31

Index 32

Chapter 1

Civic Duty and Civic Responsibility

What do supporting a **candidate** who is running for mayor, **protesting** a policy you don't agree with, and voting in the next presidential election all have in common? These are ways that citizens can get involved in local and federal government.

Participating in our government is an important part of living in a **democracy**. In democracies the people elect officials, such as mayors, governors, senators, and the president. Officials are expected to make laws and govern in ways that benefit the people they represent.

People can get involved in government in different ways. One way is to perform your civic duty. Civic duties are things that people have to do, such as paying taxes and obeying the laws. If you don't perform your civic duties you could face punishments, such as fines or criminal charges.

FACT

A democracy is not the only form of government. In some countries, people are not permitted to speak out against or question their leaders. Often they are not able to vote for their leaders. If they can vote, there may only be one candidate.

candidate—someone who is applying for a job or seeking election to an office or post
protest—to speak out about something strongly and publicly
democracy—country that has a government elected by the people

Another way to get involved is to perform your civic responsibility. Civic responsibilities are actions that you choose to do but are not required to do. Voting in an election, protesting or **boycotting** a business, and running for city council are all examples of civic responsibilities.

boycott—to refuse to buy or use a product or service to protest something believed to be wrong or unfair

What's the Difference?

It can be hard to tell the difference between civic duties and civic responsibilities. Duties are required. Responsibilities are voluntary.

Civic Duties

- - - - - - - - - - - -

- serving on a jury
- paying your taxes
- obeying the police and other law enforcement officers
- following the laws

- - - - - - - - - - - -

Civic Responsibilities

- - - - - - - - - - - -

- voting
- serving on committees and boards in your community
- picking up litter in your local park
- volunteering at an animal shelter

- - - - - - - - - - - -

Chapter 2
Civic Responsibility in Action

Speaking out about something you believe in or disagree with is an important civic responsibility. The U.S. Constitution protects your right to disagree with elected officials. Speaking out shows officials how you feel about their decisions in government.

There are many ways to speak out. You can write to or call your elected representative and share your opinion. Sometimes people will organize letter-writing campaigns about an issue such as gun control or health care.

People will then send the letters to a government official or officials at the same time. This shows that many people care about the same issue. You can also attend meetings organized by your representative, such as city council meetings. Many of these meetings are open to the public.

You also can march with others to support or protest an important issue. For example, almost 5 million people marched in cities around the world to support women's rights during the Women's March in 2017. These people didn't have to get involved. They chose to because they wanted to show their support for women's rights.

People marched in Washington, D.C., during the Women's March.

Standing Up in Ohio

Wyoming, Ohio, is a small city of about 8,500 people. In 2017 Wyoming's city council passed a **resolution** that would allow people with concealed-carry gun licenses to bring guns into city buildings. The council voted without hearing from people in the community.

Many people were angry when they heard about the resolution. They didn't want guns allowed in public buildings. Since the people elected the city council members, they felt its members needed to make decisions that reflected what the people wanted.

At the next city council meeting, members of the community filled the meeting room. They spoke out about their concerns. The city council listened and eventually **repealed** the resolution. The voices of the people in Wyoming had been heard. They had performed their civic responsibility to speak out on an issue that mattered to them.

A citizen attended a meeting at City Hall in Austin, Texas.

resolution—a formal expression of opinion, will, or intent voted on by an official body or assembled group
repeal—to officially cancel something, such as a law

The Kids of Climate Change

It's important to question our leaders — no matter how old you are. Don't be afraid to speak up and use the court system when you see injustice around you. In 2016, 21 children and teenagers from around the country filed a lawsuit against the federal government. The suit claims that the government has not protected future generations from the effects of climate change.

On April 29, 2017, people in Washington, D.C., protested the government's environmental policies. They marched from the U.S. Capitol to the White House.

Climate change is a change in Earth's normal weather patterns. The children argue that because of the government's inaction, they could experience dangerous environmental changes in their lifetimes, such as rising sea levels, toxic water and rain, and violent storms.

Chapter 3

Civic Responsibility Champions

Susanna Salter

Susanna Salter was **nominated** to be mayor of Argonia, Kansas, in 1887. During this time women were still fighting for their right to vote across the country. Women in Kansas had been granted voting rights for city elections weeks before Salter's election. Salter accepted the nomination, and she won! On April 4, 1887, Salter became the first woman to hold elected office in the United States.

Rachel Carson

You don't have to run for public office to get involved in government issues. In 1958 scientist and environmentalist Rachel Carson was studying the effects of a **pesticide** called DDT. The pesticide was used to kill insects. Carson discovered that DDT was also dangerous to plants, animals, and people. In 1962 she published her findings in the book *Silent Spring*. Because of Carson's work, DDT was banned in the United States in 1972.

A plane crew waited in a field to spray barrels of DDT in 1947. The DDT was used to kill flies.

nominate—choose someone as a candidate for a job
pesticide—a poisonous chemical used to kill insects, rats, and fungi

Harvey Milk on November 9, 1977

Harvey Milk

Harvey Milk was the first openly gay public official in San Francisco, California. In 1977 Milk won a seat on the Board of Supervisors in the city. Milk wanted to protect the rights of other gay community members. He also wanted to open low-cost day care centers for parents and help the homeless by turning old military buildings into shelters.

During this time, violence against gay Americans was common. Milk knew it was dangerous for him to hold public office, but he was determined to help his community. In 1978 Milk was shot and killed by a former member of the Board of Supervisors. Since his death, Milk has become an important symbol for the gay community. Two movies and an opera were made about his life. Every year hundreds of people promote gay rights at the Harvey Milk Festival in Sarasota, Florida.

Protesters at the No Hate rally gathered at Harvey Milk Plaza in San Francisco on August 26, 2017.

Saira Blair

Saira Blair wanted to participate in her state government. Blair ran for the West Virginia House of Delegates in 2014, when she was only 18 years old. She is a fiscally conservative Republican who wants to cut back on government spending. After winning more than 60 percent of the vote, Blair became the youngest elected public official in the United States.

Saira Blair in 2014

President Kennedy during his inauguration speech

President Kennedy and Civic Responsibility

"And so, my fellow Americans: Ask not what your country can do for you — ask what you can do for your country." —President John F. Kennedy

On January 20, 1961, John F. Kennedy was sworn in as the 35th president of the United States. In his speech to the nation, Kennedy spoke to young Americans about the benefits of public service and how it helped our country. Shortly after his election, Kennedy created the Peace Corps, an organization that sends volunteers age 18 or older to live and work in countries that need various kinds of help. In its first few months, the program received 11,000 applications from U.S. citizens wanting to join.

Chapter 4

What Can You Do?

Being a Good Citizen

You may wonder how you can help your community and government. You're too young to serve on a jury. You don't pay taxes to help improve your city streets or parks. You can't vote or get elected to government positions. But there is a big way that you can get involved. You can be a good citizen.

Imagine you are walking to school and notice one of your classmates struggling to put the chain back on his or her bicycle. Being a good citizen means stopping and helping your classmate if you can. Being a good citizen can also mean organizing a charity drive for people in need, such as people who are homeless or suffering from cancer. Recycling at home and at school is also an example of being a good citizen.

Volunteers picked up trash in an alley in Los Angeles, California.

You can help in other ways too. Even though you can't run for office just yet, you can help someone who is running. During an election season, ask a parent to march with you in a parade to support your favorite candidate. You can also volunteer to help the **campaign**. You can talk to your neighbors about why they should support your candidate. You can also write about an issue you are passionate about. You could write a letter to the editor of your local paper. Also consider writing to your senator or representative about an issue that concerns you.

campaign—series of activities organized to win an election

Don't be afraid to get involved. Remember that government officials work for the people — including you. Children can affect their community, especially when they join together.

Students talked to politicians at the Capitol building in Boise, Idaho.

An important part of being a good citizen is working to make changes that benefit others. A **petition** can be a good way to get started. Imagine that the school board has decided that all students must wear uniforms to school. You don't want to wear a uniform and neither do other students at your school. Creating a petition is one way to show your principal and the school board that many students do not want school uniforms. Petitions are formal, written requests. Typically petitions contain signatures from others who agree with your cause.

Getting Started

Before you start writing your petition, ask yourself a few questions:

* ★ What do I hope to achieve by sending this petition? Is my goal possible?
* ★ Do other students agree with my cause?
* ★ Is there any research I can do to make my argument more convincing?

petition—a document signed by many people asking leaders for a change

Writing a Petition

Now you're ready to start writing. Here are some tips to create a student petition.

Type out your goal. Include what you want to see changed and why you want this change.

Show proof. Include any research you have found to support your points.

Be respectful when you make your petition. Writing something rude or threatening won't get your point across and will most likely get you in trouble at school.

Leave room for signatures. Create a signing section for other students to print their names. Make sure to leave enough space for everyone who wants to sign.

Collecting Signatures

After you've finished writing your petition, go out there and get signatures. Log on to social media to spread your message. Work with other students to make posters supporting your opinion. Don't be afraid to talk face to face with students to explain your position and what you are trying to accomplish. You can also talk to your teachers. They may not feel comfortable signing your petition, but they may suggest other points you haven't considered.

When you are finished collecting signatures, turn in your petition to the principal or vice principal and wait for his or her response.

A student in New Mexico collected signatures for a petition.

Civic Responsibilities: How You Can Get Involved

There are other ways you can get involved. Here are some ideas to get you started. Talk to a teacher or parent to come up with even more ideas.

1. Vote in student council elections at school. Talk to your teacher about upcoming elections and how to get involved. You may even be able to run for office

2. Show respect for others. It may sound like an easy task. But showing respect for other kids and adults can make a big difference

3. Write an editorial in your student newspaper if you see something you want to change

4. Volunteer at an organization that is important to you, such as a local homeless shelter

5. Donate money you've earned to a charity. Search the Internet to find a cause you are passionate about. Your parents can help you donate

6. Encourage others to get involved in community issues and events. You and your friends can go to events as a group

7. Recycle at your school and at home. Don't throw everything into the trash. Items such as cans, bottles, paper, and cardboard can be recycled

8. Be a good neighbor by offering to walk a neighbor's dog or mow his or her lawn

9. Encourage your parents to vote. Talk to your parents about the candidates they support and the issues that are important to them

Glossary

boycott (BOY-kot)—to refuse to buy or use a product or service to protest something believed to be wrong or unfair

campaign (kam-PAYN)—series of activities organized to win an election

candidate (KAN-duh-date)—someone who is applying for a job or seeking election to an office or post

democracy (di-MOK-ruh-see)—country that has a government elected by the people

nominate (NOM-uh-nate)—choose someone as a candidate for a job

pesticide (PESS-tuh-side)—a poisonous chemical used to kill insects, rats, and fungi

petition (puh-TISH-uhn)—a document signed by many people asking leaders for a change

protest (PRO-test)—to speak out about something strongly and publicly

repeal (ri-PEEL)—to officially cancel something, such as a law

resolution (REZ-uh-loo-shuhn)—a formal expression of opinion, will, or intent voted on by an official body or assembled group

Critical Thinking Questions

1. Is serving on a jury a civic duty or civic responsibility? Why?

2. Why did Rachel Carson write the book *Silent Spring*? Use the text to help you with your answer.

3. A petition is one way to try to make a change. What is a petition?

Read More

Krasner, Barbara. *A Timeline of Presidential Elections.* Presidential Politics. North Mankato, Minn.: Capstone Press, 2016.

Kreisman, Rachelle. *Things We Do: A Kids' Guide to Community Activity.* Smart Start: Community. South Egremont, Mass.: Red Chair Press, 2015.

Zuchora-Walske, Christine. *How Can I Be a Good Digital Citizen?* Our Digital World. Minneapolis: Lerner Publishing Group, 2016.

Internet Sites

Use FactHound to find Internet sites related to this book.

Visit *www.facthound.com.*

Just type in 9781543503166 and go.

Check out projects, games and lots more at
www.capstonekids.com

Index

Blair, Saira, 18

Carson, Rachel, 15
　DDT, 15
city council meetings, 9, 11
civic duties, 5, 7
civic responsibilities, 6, 7, 8, 11,
　19, 23, 28, 29
climate change, 12–13

democracy, 4, 5

Kennedy, President John F., 19

letter-writing campaigns, 8

Milk, Harvey, 16–17

petitions, 24–27
　collecting signatures, 27
　writing, 26
protests, 4, 6, 9
　Women's March, 9

Salter, Susanna, 14

Wyoming, Ohio, 10–11